MW01706485

Life Changing *Inspirations*

By Annettee Budzban

Annettee Budzban

PublishAmerica
Baltimore

Second printing

ISBN: 1-59129-134-8
PUBLISHED BY PUBLISHAMERICA, LLLP
www.publishamerica.com
Baltimore

Printed in the United States of America

Dedication

It is with great pleasure that I dedicate this book to my special friends who have supported my writing mission. The readers of my column *Inspirations* and the many friends who encouraged me in my beginning stages of my passion to write.

You supported me by the enjoyment of your reading the things I had to write.

May we grow together in the love of Jesus Christ. I love you and deeply appreciate you.

Acknowledgment

A special thanks to my faithful husband, Jeff, who has stood by my side through thick and thin. I thank him for sharing life's journey with me. He has been a mentor and an example of how going after what you want with persistence pays off with great rewards.

His gifted hands as an artist have graced my book covers by complimenting my writings with just the right touches. They have encouraged the reader to take a peak to see what's inside.

They say, "You can't tell a book by it's cover." However in our case, I believe Jeff has done the perfect job of depicting a cover design that enhances the words from cover to cover.

Introduction

As we go through life's journey from time to time we need a word of encouragement. I found when I was in the depths of despair a timely word from our loving, heavenly Father has instructed and inspired me to have a fresh vision.

In my darkest moments I have discovered a new passion for life, as I studied the Bible and sought how God desires me to live.

I have experienced that spending a few moments each morning with Him, was just what I needed to get me through the pitfalls and potholes of life.

I compiled this book with some of my favorite inspirations so I could share with my readers the inspirational insights that have changed my life.

I encourage you to read one inspiration each week for the next year. Devote some special time to allow each message to sink deep into your heart, so it can transform your life beyond your wildest dreams!

Contents

Inspiration #1

Storing up Faith for Troubled Times

"Now faith is being sure of what we hope for and certain of what we do not see..."—Hebrews 11:1 (NIV)

"I found some nuts hidden in the basket of the barbeque grill. The squirrels must have thought it was a good hiding place," my husband said laughing, as he entered the house. A few days later as I was gazing out the window, I watched as a little gray squirrel scampered up to my flower pot on the patio. He carefully looked around before dropping a precious gem of food into the clay container. God has instilled in these precious creatures the instinct to know when and how to store up food for the long winter months ahead. Just as He has taught them to prepare for the cold hard times, He has instilled faith in our hearts so we can get through the barren seasons in our lives. We are taught as children " seeing is believing." But in the spirit realm, we believe or perceive a thing in our hearts and then we can expect to see it—that's faith. Scripture says that God has given each of us a measure of faith, Romans 12:3. Faith is like a seed, we need to plant it in our life and make it grow. Each time we step out in obedience, it increases our faith. Our faith also grows as we see God work out situations throughout our lifetime.

There are times in life when we go through trials of various types. We may feel vulnerable like we just can't make it through. God uses these trials to pull us closer to Him, so our faith will become stronger.

We do this by spending time in prayer and remembering past victories God has brought our way. When we are in between life's difficulties there are a few things we can do to store up or strengthen our faith.

1). Maintaining a consistent prayer life is a key to increasing our faith. Each time we commune with God in prayer we connect with Him in spirit, hence increasing our faith.

2). Meditating on Scripture causes the mercury of our faith to rise, because it cements God's promises in our spirits.

3). Cultivating relationships with other Christians stirs up our faith as we share the things God is doing in our lives.

We should start establishing our faith today. Believing is the key that opens the door to receiving from God.

Inspiration #2

Slow and Steady Progress Will Last in the Long Run

" Little by little I will drive them out before you, until you have increased and are numerous enough to take possession of the land."—Exodus 23:30 (AMP)

As a young newlywed, my first home was a small basement apartment. I had a second-hand double bed that someone had given to my parents. The living room area was furnished with an old sectional couch with the mid section missing from it and some scratched-up end tables that I covered with tablecloths. Then the day came to move to my first house. It was a small, two-bedroom structure that needed some work—but it was affordable and I felt blessed with it. In a few more years, I progressed to a three-bedroom ranch home with a full basement. I think you get the point here. Increase comes little by little. In the Old Testament, when the Israelites were on their way to the Promised Land they faced many obstacles. They battled war, famine, and lack. But God instructed them that they could overcome their enemies "little by little." When we are first starting out on our own, setting up a household or building a business, poverty or lack may be some of those enemies we face. Oftentimes, people want to start out big. Before long they find that making progress too fast has over-stretched their budget and gotten them into overwhelming financial burdens, leaving them with too much month at the end of the money. But the law of progress applies in this situation as well. If they tighten their spending and stay determined to watch their budget, they can turn the enemy of debt away as well. When I worked with patients who were dieting, trying to quit smoking, or working toward some other health goal, when changes were slow and steady they seemed more successful in the long run. Whatever we are lacking, whether spiritual, emotional, or physical, applying God's law of progress can bring us to increase in that area. Remembering that God's law of progress means a little at a time can keep us from giving up and help us to overcome.

Inspiration #3

Change Your Daily Tasks from Work to Worship

"Whatever you do, work at it with all your heart, as working for the Lord, not for men, since you know that you will receive an inheritance from the Lord as reward. It is the Lord Christ you are serving."—Colossians 3:23-24 (NIV)

A maid carefully stretches the corner of the sheet to fit the bare mattress. As she does she says a prayer for the safety and salvation for the next person that comes by to sleep there.

As the carpenter swings his mighty hammer and hits the nail on the head, he takes pride in doing his part to make a house for someone who might otherwise be homeless.

A young mother, patiently spends another mundane day of diaper changing and dirty laundry with a warmth in her heart that she is able to contribute to the well-being of her family.

These people hold the common bond of enjoying their daily tasks. By doing their work with an attitude to make a difference, they are honoring the Lord. Many think that worship is only when we are doing an activity that is spiritual such as reading our Bible or praying, and singing hymns at church. I had a friend tell me that she could see my work of writing devotions for God as a form of worship, but didn't connect how her task of washing dishes, and cooking meals could contribute as worship.

All our daily activity, unless it is sinful can be done for God's pleasure. We forget that God is concerned about the practical side of our life too. We grow spiritually so that it flows into the practical things we do on a daily basis, and enjoy our life the way God intended us to. When we wash our dishes, repair a car, plant a garden with an attitude of praise, it pleases God. God is the one who created us with the gifts and abilities we possess.

As unpleasant as our tasks may seem at times, a change of heart could make a difference in the way we enjoy each day. Think how happy and productive we could be, and how much it would please God, if we worshiped while we worked.

Inspiration #4

God Is Ready to Make Us Clean as Freshly Fallen Snow

"'Come now, let us argue this out,' says the Lord. 'No matter how deep the stain of your sins, I can remove it. I can make you as clean as freshly fallen snow. Even if you are stained as red as crimson, I can make you as white as wool.'"—Isaiah 1:18 (NLT)

I watched as the snow gracefully floated down to the ground. As it tumbled from the clouds above, it brought a cleansing for all the barren surroundings. Somehow, it felt refreshing to see the pure white color bath our lifeless brown tree branches and bring them to life.

The next day, as the sun glistened off the powdery snowflakes, I noticed their beauty gleam from the rooftops, snow banks, and every object within my sight. I found a new white covering hiding over the cracks in my back patio—and the surrounding gray pavement was covered with a fresh new look of whiteness and brightness as well. It was as if God had released this fresh snow fall in the midst of our drab winter days, to bring a time of refreshment. It's served to cover up the muddy ground and brighten up the bleak days of winter

God uses the symbolism of a freshly fallen snow to prove to us that the same cleansing that falls to the earth in the gloomy and barren winter season, can come to our spiritual life as well. We can become depressed and lifeless when we allow sin and guilt to overtake our souls.

By receiving Jesus Christ as our Savior, we have the freedom to come to God anytime and ask Him to forgive us, no matter what we have done. If our heart is sincere, God pardons us of our sin. Although we may not feel the immediate release, if we continue to remind ourselves that we have been forgiven, we will find that time of refreshment will start to fall on us and cleanse us like the beauty of a freshly fallen snow.

God can forgive us of sin of any size, and cover the cracks and imperfections as a result. He can transform us into something bright and new if we'll release the old sin to Him and allow Him to shower our hearts with the covering of His love.

Inspiration #5

Follow the Commandment of Love

"A new commandment I give you: love one another. As I have loved you, so you must love one another."—1 John 13:14 (NIV)

Each morning when I got up for work, as soon as my feet hit the floor, I walked directly to the kitchen. I couldn't wait to reach the refrigerator, and open the door to take a peak inside and check if my husband had packed my lunch. I smiled with delight when I spotted that little brown bag sitting on the refrigerator shelve.

I pulled out the sack to check the contents inside. Salad, a small plastic container of my favorite dressing, and some tuna. I rifled deeper through the bag searching to see if he had included my favorite item. As soon as I found it, I pulled out the small piece of paper and read the affectionate message penned on the lines for me that day. I appreciated the effort my husband put forth to acknowledge his love for me. Love takes effort. Many people think that love just comes naturally. Although some people do appear to have a bit more loving sentiment in their personality than others, it's something we all must work at. Our human nature has a tendency to be lazy. It takes energy for anyone to put forth a kindness to another.

Love isn't a feeling. It's not something you do just when you feel like it. Ask any loving parent how much effort it takes to help a child with home work after you've prepared supper and worked all day.

Love doesn't do the right thing to get something in return—love does the right thing because it is right.

Love sets us free from being selfish and self-centered. Watch how depression and discouragement leave, when you give yourself to a task that helps someone else. Showing love to one another means being courteous to people we like, as well as those we don't care for. Love was the new commandment set forth by Christ. He desired us to learn how to love, because love would obey all the other commandments.

Love isn't something we practice one special day each year. It's a discipline we put in motion each and every day of the year.

Inspiration #6

Erase Past Mistakes and Start Fresh Each Day

"The Lord is good to all and his tender mercies are over all his works."—Psalm 145:9 (AMP)

Every class room has a chalkboard. Reminiscing on my school days, I remember how each day our teacher filled the chalkboard with fascinating facts to be copied down on our papers for that day. At the end of the day when she finished the lesson, one person was chosen to wipe the chalkboard clean. I couldn't wait for my opportunity to clean the board. I took the yellow rubber eraser and passionately moved it back and forth in a smooth cleansing motion across the board until every trace of chalk was removed. I left the classroom leaving a fresh clean slate for the next day. Oftentimes, when I have a day full of regret or mistakes I like to think about the chalkboard. When I close my eyes to sleep I take the eraser and mentally erase my mistakes for the day. It helps me to wake up in the morning with a fresh new attitude.

Defeating disappointments can be hard to let go. Especially when we have done something wrong and are disappointed in ourselves. But God wants us to quickly let go of our sins, mistakes, and failures. I like to believe that the darkness that falls at the end of each day is God's way of showing us that day is dead and gone, so we can start out fresh with the next morning's sunrise.

The Bible instructs us that God's mercies are fresh every

morning. Although He doesn't condone our sins, He is quick to forgive and doesn't condemn us. He knows even when we have a heart attitude to please Him, we will make mistakes from time to time. Yet, He gives us another chance and a new opportunity for a fresh start each day.

God wants to bring new opportunities into our lives. If we want to receive the blessing and mercy of the new day set before us, we must learn to erase yesterday's mistakes from the chalkboards of our minds.

Inspiration #7

Instead of Complaining, Be Grateful for All You Have

"I have learned in whatever state I am, to be content."—Philippians 4:11 (Msg)

As a Young girl, things weren't always perfect in our household. There were bills to pay, issues to confront, and we didn't live in the lap of luxury. However, each Saturday as I would accompany my dad to run errands, whether we were at the grocery store, post office, or waiting in line to pay utility bills, whenever friends or neighbors asked him how he was, my father would always responded, "I can't complain."

We can become disillusioned with mundane tasks and issues that confront our daily lives. We stay on the lookout for the perfect circumstances to come along to bring us a spirit of contentment. However, when our circumstances don't give way to our wishes, we can find ourselves chronically complaining instead.

Complaining blocks our creativity, stifles our joy and makes the pitfalls of life appear impossible to overcome. It makes us miserable and can also cause people to want to avoid us. It zaps us of our energy and the happiness today can bring.

Because life doesn't always treat us fairly, cultivating a spirit of contentment can appear to be an illusive dream. However, the Apostle Paul encountered ship wrecks, beatings and imprisonment and yet he said that he "learned to be content."

When I face life's pitfalls and disappointments, I yearn to cultivate a spirit of contentment, instead of allowing minor incidents to place me in tailspin of constant complaining.

Contentment starts with the knowledge of God's love for us. As we pray to our Heavenly Father for the strength to calm our restless souls, we can put the learning process in motion. We need to remember that a spirit of contentment doesn't come rapidly or naturally. Developing an awareness to focus on the positive things (as few as they may be) and controlling our tongues to catch the culprit of complaint when it enters our mouth is a good place to start. Redirecting our conversation can be a beginning to cultivating contentment as an attitude of our heart.

Inspiration #8

God's Grace Can Help Us Make it Through Tough Times

"...My grace is sufficient for you, for my power is made perfect in your weakness..."—1 Corinthians 12:9 (NIV)

I remember the day well. I was rifling through the left overs in my friends refrigerator. I was grateful that she shared the remains of her wonderful home-cooked meals with me, as well as a listening ear. As I looked over the salad and other selections, I shared with her how weak I felt in managing all of the problems I was facing at the time. My friend's voice was barely within ear shot when I heard her say, "That's not at all how you appear to me. You're one of the strongest people I know."

I closed the refrigerator door and sat down on the stool at the table. I was trying to process what she just said. How could I appear to handle my problems so well when I felt so weak and overwhelmed?

That thought perplexed me for years, until one day I studied about God's grace. Then it hit me, that's how I made it through the tough times. God's power flowed through me and gave me the strength I needed to carry on in my weakness, even when I didn't realize it.

Are you going through a tough time? Do you feel like you can hardly take one more step forward? You need some of God's power (grace) to make it through.

It's our weaknesses that keep us dependent on God. God wants us to come to Him in prayer and lean on Him. When the apostle Paul was dealing with something he referred to as "a thorn in his flesh" he couldn't handle it. God reassured him "My grace is sufficient for you, for my power is made perfect in your weakness."

Grace is power we can ask God for. It's a favor that is given to us, just as a loving father provides for his child even though they don't deserve it. The good news is, we don't have to be perfect for God to extend His grace to us, because we can't improve our lives unless He gives us the power to do it.

Do you have a thorn in the flesh you're dealing with? Ask God to give you more grace to deal with it. Take that power and put in one more application. Face those hard to deal with people in your life with a loving attitude. Establish and maintain those boundaries with your rebellious teenagers. Don't be afraid to face another day because you feel helpless and alone. Even if nothing changes right away, know that you can see it through, because God's grace is flowing through you!

Inspiration #9

Creativity Can Enrich Your Spiritual Life

"You will show me the path to life; in Your presence is fullness of joy, at Your right hand are pleasures forevermore."—Psalm 16:11 (AMP)

There's nothing like a day at the beach on a warm summer day. The colorful beach towels and aroma of suntan lotion fill the sandy shores. Sunglasses, beach balls, inner tubes, plastic buckets and shovels are part of the paraphernalia you will find among the patrons.

My husband recently decided to take our little grandson for a trip to the beach. The first visit they made was only a brief one to check out the sights and a wade in the water. The next visit Jeff prepared our precious toddler with a pair of beach diapers for a brief splash. By the 3rd visit I noticed him gathering up a towel, extra pair of dry clothes, and an inflatable toy to bring along.

Jeff's adventure started out as just an ordinary visit to the beach. But as he allowed himself to become more oriented to the sights of the sun, sand, and water, he was able to make a few adjustments to enrich the pleasure in each visit and receive a fulfilling experience.

There are many benefits to be found by spending time with God—healing, strength, and comfort are a few. When we let our spiritual life become ordinary we can enjoy our time with God, but not to the fullness that He has in mind for us.

My friends have shared with me some of the inventive ways they use to enrich their time with God.

Sitting quietly on the patio or favorite park bench can stimulate the senses to the creativity and serenity of God.

Listening to soft music while praying and can make the time a soothing experience. Spending your lunch break as a date with God while you enjoy a soft drink and do your devotional reading can remind you of how special God is in your life. Staying mindful of God while puttering in the garden, reminds us that God is the Gardner of our life. Becoming creative about how to spend time with God enriches our spiritual life and makes it a pleasant and joyful experience.

Inspiration #10

When You Get Ready for the Day, Prepare Yourself Spiritually

"Stand firm then, with the belt of truth buckled around your waist, with the breastplate of righteousness in place, and with your feet fitted with the readiness that comes from the gospel of peace."— —Ephesians 6:14 (NIV)

I'll never forget the day I was preparing for my first day on the job as a nurse. For four years, I had waited for this moment. I could hardly believe my dreams were coming true.

I stood in front of the mirror and admired my brand new white uniform. It appeared so pure and fresh—it was the perfect garment for an angel of mercy.

I knew that it was customary for nurses to display their nursing school pin on their uniform. So it was with great excitement that I reached in my jewelry box and took out the small case containing my pin. I unsnapped the lid, removed the pin and placed the hard-earned token on my collar. I finagled with it a few times before I got it adjusted straight. It was with pride that I wore the silver treasure on my uniform.

However, one more thing was still needed to make my ensemble complete. I retrieved my white hat from the top shelve of the closet. It was starched and ready to go. I removed it from the Baggie and placed it on my head. It was the finishing touch. As I looked at myself in the mirror, I felt dressed for success and ready to perform my duties as a nurse.

I may have felt ready to perform my tasks, however, without my spiritual attire I'd be unequipped and fall short.

God instructs us that when we get dressed each day, we are to clothe ourselves spiritually as well. Placing on the breastplate of righteousness reminds us to make right choices and guards our hearts from the sorrows and pain wrong doing can bring. With our belt of truth fastened to us, we can bring to mind any Scriptures we may have memorized that will give us wisdom when faced with tough decisions. Slipping on our shoes of peace helps us to walk with a calm assurance everywhere we go.

With our spiritual attire in place we are empowered to perform our tasks with success each day.

Inspiration #11

Giving a Little Can Make a World of Difference

"...Afterward the disciples picked up seven basketfuls of broken pieces that were left over." —Matthew 15:37 (NIV)

We were created to make a difference. Deep inside our hearts we all yearn to accomplish something worthwhile while passing through this world. However, oftentimes, we do nothing because we think the little contribution of out time, talents or money won't amount to anything.

The recent disasters happening all over the world have given way to many people in need. But again, many times we think that if we can't join a rescue team, or give large sums of money to help out we might as well not bother.

A few weeks ago, I watched out my front window as an elderly man stooped along the side of the road picking up cans and wrappings that others carelessly threw by the wayside. I wonder if he realized what a difference his efforts made in this neighborhood.

In the biblical account in Matthew 15, Jesus had been teaching and healing a large crowd of over 4,000 people. Over the course of three days, the crowd grew tired and hungry. Jesus wanted to give them something to eat. So He asked the disciples what resources they had for food. They came up with only seven loaves of bread and a few fish. Jesus took the food and prayed over it and passed it on to the disciples to dispense out to the people. If the disciples were anything like me, I'm sure they wondered how seven loaves of bread and a few fish could feed a crowd of this magnitude. But not only did it feed the them, there were basketfuls of food left over.

Society's shortcomings can be overcome when one person is willing to make a difference. Let us be willing to work hand in hand with a mighty God who is able to multiple our meager means. We were created to be world changers. We can watch a change begin as we place our humble means into the hands of our Creative Creator—He can use our little bit to make a world of difference.

Inspiration #12

Motives Reveal Secrets of the Human Heart

"Every way of man is right in his own eyes but the Lord weighs and tries the heart."— Proverbs 21:2 (AMP)

I grew up with parents who loved to watch mystery movies. Every Sunday, Charlie Chan, Sherlock Holmes or Perry Mason visited our TV screen. Clue was also a popular game in that day and age.

The main theme of all these mysteries was who done it and why. We all watched, guessed and wondered, as clues revealed the possible motives hidden behind each suspect's story.

Motives are the thoughts behind the action. They are present in everything we do. We see people's actions on the outside, but we don't know what motivates them on the inside. Only God can search our heart and mind. He knows every thought and intent of our hearts. As far as God is concerned, our inner life reveals the real person that we are.

Have you ever thought about what your life is like on the inside? Why you do what you do?

Motives show up in our everyday actions. It's good for us to examine them. For instance, have you ever though about the presents you give? Some are given from a pure motive to bless.

But other motives for giving can include the desire to impress someone or manipulate them to do us a favor, or gain a promotion.

Self-pity can be a motive to get someone's attention or control a relationship. Having others feel sorry for us makes us think we are drawing on their affections. In reality, we need to base our relationships on mutual love, kindness and respect for each other. Without respect for each other. Without pure motives, the relationship will eventually crumble and fall.

Then there are the motives regarding our relationship to God. Do we go to church or read our Bibles to get God to love us or impress Him? He already loves us more than we'll ever know. We need to attend church and read our Bibles for our growth and to deepen our relationship and understanding of our loving Creator.

Purity of heart takes work. But when we take the challenge to examine our motives and purge our unclean actions, we will reap the blessing of serving God with a pure and blameless heart.

Inspiration #13

Life Is a Test

"But the Lord tests the heart." Proverbs 17:3

All through grade school I was a fast learner. I was in advanced classes and appeared to pass tests with a good grade average. Then I decided to enter into a new level of life. So I enrolled in Nursing school.

Eager to take one of my first exams, I made sure my number 2 pencils were sharpened and the erasers were full and intact. With pencils in hand, I approached the instructors desk and reached out to receive my copy of the test.

Settling in my seat, I said a short prayer and eagerly delved into the exam. It wasn't long and I found myself going back and forth over the answers to the questions. Passing this test wasn't as easy as I thought.

As the clock ticked away, I managed to finish just in time. I handed my test back to the instructor. Anxious to see the results, I stood in front of her as she checked it against the answer key. I quickly grew faint hearted as I watched the red check marks mount up on my paper. It didn't take me long to realize, I had failed the test.

As we advance in life we will go through many tests. Some we pass and some we fail. But life will give way to take that test again until we learn to pass it. Oftentimes, there is something greater God wants to do in our lives, but we have to go through a time of testing first. Some of the things God tests us on are faith, patience, submission to authority, and willingness to persevere.

Inspiration #14

A Majority of Life's Lessons Are Learned from Our Mistakes

"If we confess our sins, he is faithful and just and will forgive our sins and purify us from all unrighteousness."—1John 1:9 (NIV)

"I blew it!" were the words written on the front of the belated birthday card sent to me by a friend. I chuckled as I looked at the picture of white, feathery, dandelion seeds blowing from a half empty stem.

My friend usually sends me a card each year. But this year she was busy working and completely forgot about it. Although I really don't consider that by missing my birthday a mistake, her card did make me think of how serious we take things when we really have blown it. I don't know about you, but I have blown more than a few dandelion seeds from a stem. I have made more mistakes in my life than I care to think about, and I am still making them.

Oftentimes, when we make mistakes we ride the merry-go-round of guilt and condemnation as the thought "I wish I would of done this or I should of done that," flows through our mind.

But how should we feel about our mistakes, mishaps, and blunders? God wants us to be sorry for our true mistakes. We need to spend time with God and ask Him to forgive us, because Jesus died on the cross to free us from our sin and it's lasting effect.

Depending upon the severity of the wrong doing, we may experience a brief period of grief due to our actions. Sometimes, we may suffer some consequences because of what we have done. But regardless of these things, God does not want us to hate ourselves, berate ourselves, or reject ourselves. Once we have asked for forgiveness and repented for our sin, if we still experience a great amount of guilt we need to shake it off by saying, "God has forgiven me for what I have done." Sometimes, a good laugh like my friend's "I blew it" message, may help relieve some of that unhealthy guilt as well. We need to remember a majority of life's lessons will be gleaned from the mistakes we make. After we have reflected on them, we need to learn from them, and then move forward, so that we can fulfill the good plan that God has for our lives.

Inspiration #15

Words of Praise Lift and Heal Our Spirits

"Pleasant words are as a honeycomb, sweet to the mind and healing to the body."—Proverbs 16:24 (AMP)

There's nothing like a good compliment to lift your spirit. Whether read from a note or spoken, a word of praise causes your confidence to rise up, and encourages you to keep going in the right direction.

A recent TV documentary showed how positive vibrations effected the molecular construction in water. They viewed water under a microscope while someone spoke positive words into water. The molecules responded by conforming to beautiful structures that resembled snowflakes. When negative words were spoken into the water the structures formed rather jagged and distorted looking configurations.

As we apply this to human behavior, we know that when we hear negative words spoken to us, they begin to make us feel depressed and discouraged. Even when we speak them to ourselves, we start feeling miserable and defeated. But a pleasant word makes us feel victorious and confident.

In Biblical days, it was customary for the father to speak a blessing—or a compliment—over the firstborn son's life. The elderly parent would lay his hands on the eldest son's head and speak words that declared prosperity, health, and success. This spiritual tradition was so important, that in the story of Jacob and Esau, Jacob deceived his father into thinking he was his older brother so that he could receive the customary blessing from his father's positive words.

(Genesis 27) Right words can bring healing into our lives and help us to go in a right direction. Building others up with our words is one way of showing people we care. Even a reprimand can be given with a positive affirmation added.

We can see the affects words can have on our spirits, and spoken over a period of time, they can make a difference on our self-worth and value in a positive or negative way. Whether we are father's, children, wives, employers, employees, friends or others, we all need to learn to love each other with our words. We need to remember to choose our words carefully, and speak a compliment into someone's life each day.

Inspiration #16

Learn Both Your Talents and Your Limitations

"Our goal is to stay within the boundaries of God's plan for us."—2 Corinthians 10:13 (NLT)

My friend was offered a promotion and passed it up saying, "I just don't feel it's the right thing for me."I admired the fact that she knew here limitations.

Do you know your limitations? Do you understand there are some things that you just can't do, no matter how hard you try? Sometimes, it takes us a while to understand our limits.

A good friend of mine jokes that you wouldn't want to hear her sing. Yet her husband is a beautiful singer. I use to know a woman who was extremely well organized and speedy at completing her tasks. She used to get frustrated with others who couldn't keep up with her pace. She didn't realize she had the gift for speed and organization that others didn't possess—they possessed gifts that were different from hers.

There are times when we need to stretch ourselves and improve our abilities in an area; but sometimes our frustration is created by the fact that we are trying to do something we are not equipped for.

Oftentimes, people will go beyond their boundaries when the desire for prestige and pride get in the way. They find themselves frustrated, insecure, and overwhelmed. They may also be too critical of themselves. Everyone was not created to be the "janitor" or the "boss." When we start to see our abilities and limitations, we can let go of the frustration from trying to do something that doesn't fit us.

When we stay within out own niche, we find fulfillment and happiness. If we try to take on things that are not God's will for us, we will only come up with agitation and failure. God has supplied us with the talent and ability to do the job He gifted us to do. Joy and satisfaction can be found when we remain within the boundary lines of the things God has planned for us to do.

Inspiration #17

Keep a Spirit of Expectation

"Now faith is being sure of what we hope for and certain of what we do not see."—Hebrews 11:1 (NIV)

Like always, the first robin sighting and the blustery winds have signaled that spring has arrived. Although I can see a few signs of spring's presence, winter seems to be dragging it's feet in leaving. The gray barren trees can obscure one's view from the fact that spring is already here.

The trees appear lifeless, as they collect sap over the cold winter season to help them bloom leaves in the spring. Then at just the right time when the sunlight hits them, tiny buds protrude, followed by plenty of green leaves. Multi-colored flowers start to push their way through the ground, as it is softened by the spring rain. God has planned the precise way and time to let spring come forth.

The expectancy of spring is a wonderful example of the way the spirit of God moves in our lives. Sometimes we go through a long dull season of what we may call winter in our lives. During this time our lives may seem dull, or dreary while we wait for the fulfillment of our dreams.

While we are waiting for a change to take place, just as the sap collects in the trees over the winter months, attitudes build up in our hearts. Sometimes we collect bitterness. Other times, it may be envy, fear, or negativity of some sorts. We may feel a spirit of defeat creeping in. God wants us to build trust in Him and Jesus our Savior, and collect faith, hope, and love. He wants our hearts to fill with an expectancy that He will come to our aid in some way. And at the right time just as the sunshine hits the tree branches and spring shows forth, the expectancy in our hearts will spring forth some newness in our life.

Having faith and expectancy means we can't see with our eyes what we are believing for because it's still formed as a dream in our hearts. But just as we can expect that spring is on the way, if we strive to keep our dream alive, our faith will produce the things that our eyes have not yet seen, but our hearts have hoped for.

Spring is a time for expectancy. As we wait for the refreshment springs beauty brings, let's ask God to help us fill our hearts with anticipation and expect our dreams to come true.

Inspiration #18

Pencil in Some Time for Relaxation

"Thus the heavens and earth were completed in all their vast array. By the seventh day God had finished the work he had been doing; so on the seventh day he rested from all his work."— Genesis 2:1,2 (NIV)

For his birthday, I bought my husband a bench to set on our front porch. Recently, when the sky was blazing in a sunset of orange, red, and purple hues, he left his projects in the garage and headed for the bench.

I watched from the front door as he leaned back and folded his hands across his chest. The sky was his focus as he relaxed and gazed at the fabulous color painted across the horizon.

"That should be our sunset bench." I said, as I peaked my head out the front door. He agreed that having a special place to relax and enjoy God's creation was a great idea.

When was the last time you sat back and relaxed? With the beautiful, sunny summer days ahead, have you penciled in any time for relaxation on your calendar? I'm not talking about an action-packed vacation. I'm talking about a slow paced swing in the hammock type of day. A day, or even a few moments, where you can relax and sit and enjoy the beauty of all God created. We can get caught up in paying our bills, improving our homes and working to make ends meet, that we forget to take a step back and enjoy all the beauty God has given us in our natural surroundings. Since we follow God's example, finding some time of solitude and rest to enjoy the beauty of a sunset, the color scheme of a rainbow, or the reflection of the sunlight sparkling off the refreshing lake waters, should be part of our routine. After God created all the vast array of the heavens and earth, He sat back, rested and marveled at what he had accomplished. He enjoyed all the work of His hands. I think He must have smiled brightly.

Why not enjoy life's journey and not just the final destination? Following God's example to build a time for rest into our schedules will help us to enjoy creation and energize our souls.

I pray you can find some time to discover the joy of relaxation and the pleasure of God's handiwork—it's a blessing from above.

Inspiration #19

Compliments Work Wonders on the Soul

"A word aptly spoken is like apples of gold in settings of silver."—Proverbs 25:11 (NIV)

I recently received an e-mail from an old childhood friend who found me through an Internet search. A huge smile crossed my lips as I looked over her praiseworthy words for my mother. I carefully read through the words she wrote that went something like this:

"I remember the canned red-fruit punch your mother bought, and the kind heart she had to allow you to share it with me." Compliments keep our hearts tender, and energize our souls. They don't just nurture the recipient, but have a special way of strengthening the soul of the giver as well.

Compliments can be words of praise, such as "I like your new car; The way you wear your hair; your knack for understanding me warms my heart; or, job well done!" They can also be given as a formal act of courtesy, when we esteem the hostess of a dinner party regarding the tasty meal, or thank a store clerk for good service.

Gracious words are so important to our well-being, that experts say that the average employee is not just interested in being paid a decent wage, but desires to be given a word of admiration regarding their work when handling the job well.

In our modern culture, words offered out are oftentimes offensive, harsh, or arrogant, yielding results that are contrary and counterproductive, rather than kind-hearted compliments which build our well-being and foster productivity. Uncomplimentary words cause us to become harsh, bitter, and uncaring, ruining our relationships with others and tearing down the best of marriages, business partnerships, and parent-child bonding.

God wants us to speak words that will bring life to the souls of those around us. We may not like everything about a person, but if we look close enough, we may find there is something we can openly admire about them. Just think how offering kind words will actually help them look forward to seeing us, rather than running the other way. Why not sharpen our word skills and build a relationship as we compliment someone today?

Inspiration #20

Enjoy the World Around You with a Childlike Faith

"But Jesus called the children to him and said, "'Let the little children come to me, and do not hinder them, for the kingdom of God belongs to such as these. I tell you the truth, anyone who will not receive the kingdom of God like a little child will never enter it.'"—Luke 18: 16,17 (NIV)

I was looking out the front window. I watched as the sun slowly set on the longest day of the year. I twisted the wand to close the blinds on the picture window, then walked toward the kitchen.

From the back window, I saw something twinkle in the air. It flashed brightly again. I realized I was seeing my first firefly for the year. I watched closely as several lightening bugs winked and blinked, flashing like delightful little night lights, flittering their wings, and lighting their way through the dark space of my backyard.

I pondered the moments I spent as a young girl, watching in amazement as they revealed their God-given fireworks display, in conjunction with the celebration of the Fourth of July holiday.

Watching fireflies again, reminded me of the faith a young child possesses. A child's faith is a trusting faith. It doesn't reason and make all sorts of excuses like our natural thinking process. It simply believes what it knows to be true but cannot see.

Have you ever pondered what child-like faith is? It is the same kind of faith we use to trust the sun to rise and set each day. It believes electricity to appear each time we flip the switch—as long as the bill has been paid, of course. It doesn't understand the emotion of love, but believes it exists. Sometimes, life's problems harden our hearts and we refuse to see the wonder of creation or the possibility of a problem to be resolved.

Child-like faith relieves stress, as it places it's trust in God to bring about answers and solutions. God doesn't expect us to cast our responsibility, or function like a child. He desires that we abandon our worries and cares and believe for Him to work them out, with the same trust a child does.

Jesus said we could never enter into the kingdom of God if we don't possess this child-like faith. Faith is a spiritual principle God set in motion. It helps us believe Jesus Christ died for our sin, and for God to fulfill His other promises for our lives, as well.

In these turbulent times, let's enjoy the world around us and enter into God's plan for our lives with a child-like faith today.

Inspiration #21

True Friends Hold You Accountable for Your Actions

"Oil and perfume rejoice the heart; so does the sweetness of a friend's counsel that comes from the heart."—Proverbs 27:9 (AMP)

Several years ago, I was complaining about the health issues I was dealing with. A good friend of mine confronted me and told me that I needed to change my focus. At first I felt wounded by her confrontation. I thought she was very insensitive to my problem. But after giving her advice some thought, I started to see threads of truth in the caring suggestion she gave me. That advice changed my whole perspective. My life greatly improved as I started to make the best of my situation.

A few years ago, a friend was having problems in her marriage. She shared with me how another man was starting to pay attention to her. I warned her that she would only be inviting trouble into her life if she were to get involved in an affair. After pondering my advice, she placed her focus back on her marriage and working things out.

To let a friend do something harmful without trying to stop them is to hurt them rather than help them. To confront them in a loving way to do what is right is known as accountability.

Accountability has been an established part of many helps programs. Anyone who has ever been in a drug or alcohol rehabilitation program knows that part of successful treatment means partnering with someone who will help keep you accountable to your goal. People desiring to lose weight, oftentimes, join programs with a group of people that will keep them accountable.

However, don't get confused here; keeping someone accountable does not mean controlling them or pointing out every fault and flaw they have. It means when you see they are in harm's way, advising them in the right direction in a caring, gentle manner.

God expects us to love each other enough to keep one another liable. He has given us truth to transform our lives. When we need an extra boost of support, let's ask God to surround us with friends that will hold us accountable to maintain Godly integrity. It's good to have someone who will direct us to the path that leads to a better life.

Inspiration #22

Where Is God in the Midst of Tragedy and Sorrow?

"My God, I called to you for help."—Psalm 30:2 (NIV)

Have you ever looked around you at the turmoil in the world and wondered, where is God? Maybe you've experienced some tribulation of your own and questioned if God was aware of your problems.

Just recently, my husband went to the hospital for surgery. My previous nursing experience reassured me it was a fairly common procedure; yet, I knew there was always the possibility of a complication. I was housebound due to an illness and unable to be with him at the hospital. This factor made me a bit more uneasy; each day before the surgery I did my best to place it in God's hands.

The morning of the operation, a good friend of my husband's picked him up and took him to the hospital. After he left, I spent some time in prayer and did my best to cast my concern on the Lord, as the Bible says to do in 1 Peter 5:6,7.

When I looked at the clock and noticed it was time for Jeff's surgery, tears streamed down my cheeks as I longed to be at my husband's side. Then in a split second, I started to recognize God's love and the many ways He revealed Himself in our situation.

I realized what a blessing it was that my husband's friend could take him to the hospital and be by his side. I found comfort in knowing one of the pastors from our church went up to pray with my husband before the procedure. God provided my niece, who is a nurse, to be available that day to go up to the hospital and help get Jeff settled in his room and called me with pertinent information. Many caring friends, prayed, called or e-mailed that day. I could see God's hand at work.

When we think God has left us in a tough spot or wonder why He doesn't feed the hungry, care for sick and tend to the tragedy's of the world we should take another look. God works through people. He gave humanity the authority to "rule" and "subdue" the earth (Genesis 1:27, 28.) Although, God can and does work a miracle at any given time, He's always working miracles through the hands of people—if we will let Him.

Inspiration #23

Everything You Do in Life Is a Choice, So Choose Well

"See, I set before you today life and prosperity, death and destruction."—Deuteronomy 30:15 (NIV)

Did you eat breakfast this morning, or did you decide to skip it? Did you call in sick because you went to bed late last night and didn't feel like getting out of bed this morning?

Did you speak a kind word to your spouse or child, or where you so busy getting ready that you didn't to say anything to them? When you went out shopping, did you use some restraint and pass up charging that item you just "had to have" but don't really need, or did you buy it anyway?

Have you ever stopped to realize that everything you do in life is a choice? Even when you decide to do nothing about a situation you are still making that choice.

Each day you choose how you are going to spend your money. You decide whether or not to nurture a relationship. You determine if you want to stay at the job you hate, or move on to one you might like. You make choices regarding your health by what you eat, or don't eat. And you decide to bear grudges against people or circumstances rather than let go of all the negativity you feel.

God has a lot to say about choice. We can make a choice that brings life—in other words work toward a positive outcome—or we can choose death—which results in negativity and fosters outcomes that brings pain and misery….God says it's up to us.

It's true that oftentimes, life throws you some things that are totally unfair. But how you handle it is a choice you make.

"Choosing life," is to pursue your God-given dreams: to foster a close relationship with God, to treat people with kindness——even when it hurts, to develop beauty both inside and out, to give up a mediocre lifestyle and pursue excellence in all that you do.

The power to choose is a God-given gift to help you live out your dreams. You don't have to take giant leaps of faith. You can start by doing small things first. That, oftentimes, gives you the courage to make a bigger step.

Why not pray and ask God what new choices you can make; help combat some of the destructive consequences from making unhealthy ones.

Inspiration #24

Spiritual Direction Can Help You Handle Times of Stress

"Come to Me, all you who labor and are heavy-laden and overburdened, and I will cause you to rest. (I will ease and relieve and refresh your souls.)"—Matthew 11:28 (AMP)

I recently replaced my oak kitchen chairs. Over time, the glue in the joints dried up and the chairs started to weaken. They just didn't do the job of bearing a persons weight as they should.

When someone would sit on them, they would creak and wobble. I was afraid they'd fail to support the person as they should, and collapse under the stress.

Stress—it's a word we hear often in our culture. I heard the word was originally developed as an engineering term to describe the amount of strain a physical structure could take without collapsing under pressure—like my kitchen chairs.

As a nurse, I used the word "stress" when assessing factors that may have attributed to a persons illness. Stress is a major cause, or aggravating factor in 70 percent of disease. It not only relates to the physical aspect of a person's burden, but includes the emotional and mental factors as well.

God has designed us to tolerate a certain amount of stress. It's what motivates us to get things done. But when we accumulate an unreasonable amount, it starts to show up in our physical, emotional, and spiritual well-being.

Almost anything can become a stressor. Health-care professionals have a list and score stress. A few factors on the list include a marriage or a move, the loss of a spouse through death or divorce, worry and anxiety over a “to do” list that never ends, unresolved relationship issues, financial distress, or other concerns that continue on for a prolonged period of time.

Health experts may advise rest, counseling or medication; but we must seek spiritual direction as well. Jesus tells us to come to Him with our burdens. How do we do that? Prayer is a key. God knows us better than anyone. Verbalizing our concerns to Him and listening for any advice is important.

Advice may come through a creative idea or an insight, an article or a book with a topic of interest might catch our attention. God may show us how to change our schedule, or handle a relationship. Acting in obedience to whatever insight we receive is an important aspect of the remedy. While we wait for results, praying for strength and counting our blessings—instead of stressing—can help us cope with the pressure in our daily lives.

Inspiration #25

In Stormy Times, Hospitality Can Be a Saving Grace

"Offer hospitality to one another without grumbling."—1 Peter 4:9 (NIV)

As the dark clouds loomed overhead, my friend realized the storm warnings for her neighborhood were more than mere predictions. She voiced concern when she heard that damaging tornadoes were among the forecast as well.

Many years had come and gone without trace of a twister in their town. But as the torrential rains poured down and the winds fiercely blew, tree limbs and debris started falling, and fears started rising. Within half an hour, streets lights dangled from the top of their posts. Power lines lay on the rain soaked ground. Rooftops were tattered and torn off. Hearts were heavy, as they realized the damage the storms and winds brought to this modest little town.

Power outages were apparent, as the sweltering heat soon replaced the comfort of the air-conditioned buildings. My friend's husband started up the small generator they had on hand. Running her fan for a breath of fresh air and keeping their food from spoiling were among her many concerns.

Several days went by without electricity being restored. My friend watched from her window as workers sweated around the clock to replace fallen power lines.

As the days went by, her concerns for her neighbors grew. How could they afford to travel to the other side of town, and pay for the cost of three meals a day, with a family consisting of several members? Many neighbors thought of utilizing their charcoal grills, but their use was forbidden due to potential fire hazards. However, she pondered, her gas grill wouldn't be a problem.

Spirits rose as she invited the neighbors for a cookout. Between what she could provide, and what others pitched in, there was plenty of food for everyone. As meat sizzled on the grill, various aromas soared through the air. It was a great time of sharing food and fellowship—just like an old-fashioned block party.

A bad situation turned out for the better, simply because a bit of hospitality was offered. When God placed the gift of hospitality within us, He knew the many ways it could be utilized. When difficulties arise we can place our grumbling aside and take a moment to ponder how we could offer some hospitality and help one another.

Inspiration #26

Consider Laughing Matters When Facing Adversity

"...He who has a glad heart has a continual feast (regardless of circumstances)."—Proverbs 15:15 (AMP)

Have you had a good laugh today? Maybe your heart is heavy over some circumstance that is stopping the flow of laughter in your life. There are times I struggle with that too. That's why I ask God, "Teach me to laugh."

Laughter is produced from a heart that is overflowing with joy. Oftentimes, we feel like there is no joy within us. Proverbs 15:15 reveals that God has placed joy in the heart of every believer (my paraphrase). But it's up to us to cultivate it. How do we do that?

Norman Cousins was diagnosed with cancer. When he was given a grim report, he decided to fill the rest of his days with laughter. He watched funny movies and an amazing thing happened—he laughed his way to health!

I'm not saying we will all have the exact same result if we do this, But there is a principle about laughter. In the Biblical days of old, men of war use to stop up the wells of their enemy by filling them with rocks and dirt so no water could flow through them. When Abraham's enemy, the Philistines, blocked up his well, God used Isaac—whose name means laughter—to open his well back up.

When the wells of our hearts are filled with sorrow, depression, and pain, it blocks our flow of laughter. Laughter is one way to take charge of our heart and fill it with cheer.

Movies, joke books, and a fun time with friends are a few activities that can accomplish this.

As we learn to laugh, staying mindful of following the Biblical guidelines for no "obscenity, foolish talk, or coarse joking." (Ephesians 5:4) can make our joy a time of pure fun. Making another person the brunt of our jokes, spewing crude remarks, or spouting obscenities are not considered laughing matters to God.

Although laughter is good, it's not realistic that we should laugh about everything; but a good chuckle should be a part of our daily lives. Being joyful in life's journey doesn't mean the absence of problems, rather, practicing God's principles in the presence of them.

Inspiration #27

Learning to Receive Is a Gift We Give to Ourselves

"...Which is greater: the gift, or the alter that makes the gift sacred?"—Matthew 23:19 (NIV)

I remember, as a young girl, the excitement of my first gift exchange. Each day before school started, I stood outside the window of my second grade classroom, looking at the packages surrounding the base of our class's Christmas tree. I shifted my feet back and forth, and rubbed my hands together, as the cold December air nipped at my toes and fingers. My heart remained warmed, however, as I stared through that window and dreamed about the contents wrapped inside each pretty colored package neatly trimmed with ribbons and bows. Each day my anticipation grew for the great day we would exchange our gifts.

It was the last day of school before our Christmas break. As soon as we finished lunch recess, the party began. As the gift tags were read aloud, each present was passed out to its recipient. My heart pounded with excitement as I carefully removed the festive paper. It was a book of poetry. I wasn't so sure what I thought of this gift. I loved to read, but as a child I wasn't expecting anything quite so practical. All around me I could hear the moans and groans of other disgruntled gift receivers, as well.

As the years went by, I attended many parties that included the exchange of gifts. Sometimes, I received with joy, when the gift was something I had longed for. But other times, I was disgruntled, when my heart sunk with disappointment over a gift I didn't like or felt I had no use for.

Then I had a change a heart when the Lord revealed to me it's a prideful heart that doesn't receive a gift with joy or gratitude. I needed to humble my heart, and allow the giver to receive the blessing from their giving. When I came across this Scripture I saw that it is not the gift itself that matters—but the alter, the mode of transportation by which it is was given—that is the giver's heart.

This doesn't mean we cannot make suggestions to someone we will receive a gift from, or even exchange a gift given to us. It doesn't mean we have to give a gift in return. But we must remember others prove their love for us by their act of giving. The gift we give them in return is a humble heart ready to receive. Then we have allowed them the blessing of giving.

Jesus Christ gave His life for our eternal salvation. If we haven't done so, let's consider humbling our hearts and receive Him, as our Savior, God's gift of love this Christmas.

Inspiration #28

Repentance Is a Blessing That Leads to Restoration

"If you repent, I will restore you."—Jeremiah 15:19 (NIV)

It's that time of the year, once again. The time we sit back and get our list of resolutions started for the next year. As we watch the shiny ball slowly drop down the tower in Time Square signaling the midnight hour, we feel the pressure mounting to try our resolution again, and this time get it right!

What makes us come back to that point year after year? I believe God places that desire within us. It's called repentance.

Repentance—it's one of those Biblical terms we often shake our heads at trying to understand. What does it mean to repent? It means to realize we're headed in a wrong direction and decide to change our ways.

It's a repentant heart that decides to believe Jesus Christ was sent as a sacrifice for our sins—and as we believe in Him we are forgiven and receive a restored relationship with God. But our repentance doesn't stop there. A repentant heart sees the need to continue making improvements as we go through life's journey. It feels the tugging of the Holy Spirit leading us to take responsibility and discover a way that will restore and improve the quality of our life.

If you and I want to be blessed, we must make it our aim to pursue a life that's pleasing to God.

Deciding to take responsibility to care for our bodies by removing habits that have the potential to destroy us can improve our health and help us have the strength and longevity to fulfill God's purpose for our lives. Resolutions to manage our money wisely can help us overcome the burden of financial worries. As we utilize our time better, we can receive the benefits of having a well-balanced and fulfilled life as we manage time for God, family, and recreation.

However, the decision starts with us. Repentance is a blessing that leads to restoration. All God requires of us is a repentant heart and willingness to change our ways.

As we start our list of resolutions this year, lets take it to God and ask for His forgiveness for our slack and to help us bring about change in that area of our lives. It's doing right that helps us gain that sense of fulfillment we are looking for. With God's help and a repentant heart, we can take some action and find some satisfaction this new year.

Inspiration #29

True Success Comes from the Knowledge of God

"My people are destroyed for lack of knowledge."—Hosea 4:6 (NIV)

Something inside each of us whispers we are destined for greatness. We have the longing deep within our hearts to do something outstanding, but sometimes we are ignorant in our understanding of how to fulfill the desire.

God created man for great things. Looking back at the past 100 years, we witness how man's greatness has been revealed, when we enjoy the convenience of modern inventions

However, our search for greatness, oftentimes, guides us in all the wrong places. Mislead youths might join in gang activities looking for power, prestige, and a sense to belong to something.

Young girls may abandon their dignity when their search for love gets them entangled with the deceptive thinking that they must attract the opposite sex with seductive glamor; before you know it, wrong perceptions manifest themselves in eating disorders, and the wearing of inappropriate attire develops out of a deep need to be desired and cared for.

One of the most prominent figures of the Bible, was a man named Moses. As Moses grew he too knew God was calling him to do something great with his life. Then one day he realized the dream in his heart was to become a leader and free the Israelites from their slavery in Egypt. So, when he saw an Egyptian fighting with an Israelite, Moses decided to defend the Israelite by murdering the Egyptian. After that, he realized what he had done was wrong—he hadn't handled the situation with wisdom. Fleeing for his own life and searching for a new start, he wandered away and spent forty years in the desert learning the ways of God, and cultivating a new way of thinking. Then he went back and became the dynamic leader God intended him to be.

Oftentimes, in our desire for greatness we are like Moses; we feel the desire to express the greatness within our hearts, but go about accomplishing it in misguided ways, rather than utilizing the wisdom of God.

Without the wisdom to hold a marriage together, cultivate friendships, minister to others, our lives are empty and futile. Our souls are destroyed, as we push aside the love of God and family for more power, wealth, and fame.

True success, comes from the knowledge of God. It keep us from perishing, and fosters us to flourish. Godly wisdom keeps us from destructive mind sets and helps us find the love, power, and significance we are all searching for.

Inspiration #30

Accepting Criticism Helps Us Grow

"If you reject criticism, you only harm yourself, but if you listen to conviction, you grow in understanding."—Proverbs 15:32 NLT

During my years as a nurse manager, I had the task of doing annual evaluations of each staff member. I was administered a standard form to use for writing out each employee's evaluation. At the end of each form was a place to list areas where the worker was strong or needed some improvement. This was so they could establish a goal.

Oftentimes, I let the employee decide their strengths and weaknesses. But there were many times they just couldn't think of any goals or areas that needed improvement. When this occurred, I had to assess their work performance and make a suggestion as to what I thought they could improve in. I tried to make the suggestion as positive as possible so they could see the possibilities that could come about if they would strive to comply. Sometimes my suggestions were met with resistance. They took the constructive criticism as a personal assault, rather than a helpful tip to inspire them be their best. I know there have been times when I, too, have received a constructive correction with the wrong perspective. Let's face it. It's human nature to feel rejected when someone points out our flaws.

God instructs us that if we are wise,we will examine all criticism that comes our way and discern if it is a wise suggestion, or a harsh accusation. It's true that not all criticism that comes our way fits our situation. But if we keep an open mind and a humble heart we can grow in leaps and bounds when we take constructive criticism to heart.

There are many times I have improved greatly when I have swallowed my pride, and met with the suggestions given me.

When constructive criticism is given and taken in the wise context in which was meant, we can accomplish great goals and improve our lives.

Inspiration #31

God Shows Us His Kindness and Blesses Our Lives

"...he Lord make His face to shine upon and enlighten you and be gracious (kind, merciful, and giving favor) to you..."——Numbers 6:25 (AMP)

Last Saturday my husband spent the day helping a friend of his move. He and a couple other men, spent a few hours emptying the two-car garage of its tools, packed all the paraphernalia in boxes, and loaded up the 20-foot truck. Then they drove 2 hours away so they could unload the multiple boxes, snow shovels, and rest of the tools. These men did this for free. They gladly spent their time and energy doing a favor for a friend.

Have you ever needed a favor from a friend? Sometimes we just need someone to come along side of us and help us out. There's nothing like someone just doing us a favor.

A favor isn't something we earn or deserve; it's something someone does for us with no strings attached. One of the dictionary definitions of favor says: "To do a kindness for." Have you ever asked anyone to do a favor or kindness for you?

God is in the business of showing us His kindness. Sometimes, I pray that God will give me favor when I need some help with something. I ask God to give me favor and send the help I need.

Sometimes, when we need a new job, a raise, or a new friend, we can ask God to grant us favor. When we go on that interview that is so important, we can ask God for approval above the other applicants. It is God's will to bless us. Now, I'm not saying this will always get us whatever we want. But when we need some extra help, it doesn't hurt to ask.

The Bible mentions several places that God will give us favor. When I was a young girl our pastor spoke the Scripture in Numbers 6:25 over the congregation each week before we left the church sanctuary. He wanted God's blessing, and kindness to shine upon His congregation. Whatever your struggle, reach out to God and ask Him to show you some favor this upcoming week.

Inspiration #32

Taking the Hard Road Can Lead to a More Fulfilled Life

"Enter through the narrow gate. For wide is the gate and broad is the road that leads to destruction, and many enter through it. But small is the gate and narrow the road that leads to life, and only a few find it."—Matthew 7:13-14 (NIV)

Several years ago, I took a vacation with my husband to see the mountains in Colorado. I couldn't wait to see the view from a majestic mountaintop. Since we were both licensed drivers, we decided to take turns driving and make the 16 hour trip straight through.

As Jeff slept in the passenger seat, I turned on the setting for the cruise control, and enjoyed driving on the Interstate. There were many wide lanes all around me, so the traveling was smooth and easy. I cruised for hours. However, as we approached the mountains of Colorado, the driving wasn't so smooth and easy anymore, so I quickly switched places with Jeff who was more experienced at driving on the mountain roads.

The spectacular mountain view I had anticipated, was somewhat skewed by the narrow, mountain passages we traveled. The curvy twists and turns demanded great concentration by the driver. As I looked at the shoulder of the road, I noticed only a few inches of gravel between the road and the mountain edge it separated. At that moment, I was more impressed by my husband's ability to drive on these narrow mountain passages. As I looked down I realized one slip, and you could fall. It was quite different than the ease experienced while cruising on the wide highways the Interstate had offered.

Jesus mentioned in Matthew 7:13-14 there were two roads in life that we can choose which hold the same contrast as the drive on the narrow mountain passage, and the broad highway I experienced.

We can travel the broad road with ease. It doesn't require much concentration to details and can easily lead us into destruction, because we are not paying attention to the little things that improve our life.

The travelers on the narrow road, pay much more attention to the details that really matter in life. They choose Jesus as their Savior, and are prayerful and careful to do the things that will promote and create a good life. They know cultivating a relationship with God, and following key principles like loving each other, giving, caring for someone else, and treating others with kindness, will get them further in this life than cheating, stealing and being rude.

They also take care of their bodies so they can be healthy and fulfill God's plan. Financial planning is a part of their daily lives so they don't spend tomorrow's prosperity, today, and find themselves poverty stricken.

Life's carefree highway can often be deceiving, because it doesn't require much discipline. Paying close attention to the needs of others, and the details in our lives, can help us to discover a what life is all about.

Inspiration #33

Ultimate Gardener Knows What Is Best: Allow Room for Growth

"...every branch that does bear fruit He prunes so it will be more fruitful."—John 15:2 (NIV)

I noticed thin, wispy branches sprouting all over the trunk of our weeping willow tree. It seemed as if these branches appeared overnight.

Just last fall we had the tree professionally trimmed. They pruned off several of the lower branches, and thinned out the ones on the tree's top. When they were finished, it looked well groomed and allowed more sunlight to flow into the backyard.

Now all of a sudden, branches are budding all around the trunk of the tree. As I examined the sudden growth spurt, I remembered the concept behind pruning trees. I'm not a gardener, nor do I possess much of a green thumb. However, I have heard some facts about the pruning of trees. It's my understanding that pruning is done to cut off the parts of the tree that are dead or causing overgrowth. There is not room for the healthy new branches to come in when overgrowth is apparent. Once that is done, the tree is left healthy and vibrant. However, the lopping off the overgrowth causes new growth to occur; so once the tree is pruned, it starts to flourish. I guess one could surmise from my willow's new sprouts, that it is flourishing from last year's pruning. There was nothing unhealthy about my willow tree; it just had a some overgrowth. Too much of a good thing. Sometimes, in our lives, we may be healthy and going in the right direction, but we may be doing too much, or we may need to let go of a few things in order to keep going in the right direction.

The Bible says God is a gardener. He uses gardening analogies to give us examples about our lives. Just like a Gardener prunes the trees, God may prune off a few things for our good or He may ask us to apply some self-discipline and prune them back ourselves. Sometimes the things that need to go may not be bad for us; they just might not be God's best.

Letting go of a friendship that has been cut off, eliminating a few activities to allow more time for something better, or learning to say no to things you don't feel inspired to do can be healthy ways of pruning back things that aren't necessarily bad, but just not the best. Then we allow room for some new things to grow in our lives.

Inspiration #34

Don't Be Deceived by the Allure of Sin in Your Life

"You relied on oppression and depended on deceit, this sin will become for you like a high wall cracked and bulging, that will collapse in an instant."—Isaiah 30:20 (NIV)

Over the years, some of the fun summer activities I have enjoyed include carnivals, amusement parks, and county fairs. I imagine you have too.

There's nothing like going on rides that tickle your innards and make you laugh. You might also enjoy the challenge of a game that tests your skill and ability; or wonder what prize you might win after choosing your favorite duck from the duck pond. You can even excuse your manners, as you lick the gooey, cotton candy from your fingers.

But then there are the places that can delude the mind and stir up fears; like the compromising places in the fun house.

Fun houses include all sort of challenges that deceive the naked eye. As a young girl, I marveled the first time I gazed at my reflection in one of those funny distorted mirrors. One made my body look short and fat; another made me appear tall and sleek. They appeared so real that if I didn't know any better, I could have easily been deceived believing I was looking at my own reflection.

A trip inside the fun house includes optical illusions as well. Sometimes rooms appear larger than they really are, or smaller than tend to be. Other times they cause you to crawl on your knees through a dimly lit hallway, twisting your body to try to make your way through a narrow passage. The deceptions can be challenging and fun.

The analogy of deception that the fun house reveals can be a great reminder of how the sin in our lives can appear enjoyable too. That's the delusion—we think we're having a fun time, because our vision of what reality is has been distorted. But in the end when our delusion collapses, we discover the deception of enjoyment only led to our destruction.

Deceptions in our minds can spring from many causes, addictions handed down from our parents, misconceptions of what life is all about, things others have said to us to tear down our self-worth, and lies Satan has enticed us to believe. However, gazing into the mirror of the truth of God's Word can reveal them to us, and remove us from deceptions destruction effects.

I think a trip to the fun house might be all the fun and enjoyment we need when it comes to allowing our minds to be deceived.

Inspiration #35

God's Gift of Life Is What You Make of It

"...I have set before you life and death, blessings and curses. Now choose life."—Deuteronomy 30:19 (NIV)

"Life is what you make it!" was something my father use to say. Sometimes when I was bored or wanted to sulk in self-pity over my problems, he would often give me that advice. Many times I just wanted to reply, "That's your opinion," and ignore his advice and sulk in my bad mood.

However, I have discovered that what my father said is true. As a matter of fact, our heavenly Father gives us the same advice. He gave us the right of choice.

We can choose a good attitude. Sometimes, we have multiple issues that are weighing heavy on our hearts. Many may be serious. We can't seem to get our minds off of our troubles. But we can choose to find some bright spots to relieve our troubled minds and motivate us to make something better come from the circumstances surrounding us. We can choose to live with passion, or down and depressed which deadens our joy.

We can choose to ask God for help. The Scriptures explain that sometimes we don't receive because we don't ask God. We should examine if we have asked Him to help us make right choices and to remain joyful; He is always ready and waiting for us to ask for His help.

We can make the choice to accept ourselves for the person God created us to be, rather than continually going over our deficits and shortcomings. We all need to make improvements, and repent of sin, but we can't continually beat ourselves up over them.

We can choose to be content with what we have and take good care of it. This makes us good stewards over what God has given us; if He sees we desire to take care of what we have, He can delight in giving us more.

We can choose to achieve. Keeping a desire alive for self-improvement is a good step in making our lives better. In this day and age, with libraries, Internet access, and learning channels we have a wealth of knowledge at out fingertips. God tell us He gave us the ability to create wealth. We can enrich our attitudes, and gain skill and talent through knowledge and hard work.

We can choose eternal life by receiving Jesus Christ as our Savior.

God wants us to have a good life and points out we have the right to choose. Since life is what we choose to make it, why not make the choice to take some steps to cultivate a better one.

Inspiration #36

Divine Communication Doesn't Need Technology

"I call on you, O God, for you will answer me; give ear to me and hear my prayer."—Psalm 17:6 (NIV)

I had a friend recently ask me how she could contact me. She inquired if I have an e-mail address, Web site, fax, cell phone, or other means of communication.

In this day and age, we have multiple ways people can contact us. Cell numbers are popular; so is text messaging. Many still have our house phones and others have fax machines in their home offices. But even though we have the means for several types of contact, there are still times we get someone's voice mail, or experience the frustration of getting cut off in the middle of a conversation wondering if the other person can still hear us.

It's comforting to know communicating with God is much easier than trying to get a hold of our earthly friends. God is omnipresent, which means He is everywhere. He is also omnipotent, which means He is powerful. He is not too busy running the universe to hear our requests as some believe. He has time for each one of us. He doesn't place us on hold or ask us to leave a message on His answering machine. He hears us when we call Him.

When it comes to communing with God, we can be glad we don't have to contend with any of the barriers that keep us from connecting with others. Wherever we are we can just say the name of Jesus, and discuss what's on our hearts; then stretch our faith to believe that He hears us. The closest our modern technology comes to comparing how we commune with God is the utilization of a walkie-talkie. This provides instant communication with the recipient as it directly connects you to the other person. The difference is, however, with God we don't need a signal, we just speak and are directly connected with Him. The spiritual workings of it are a mystery to us.

God is available to talk with us anytime of the day or night. If we search the Scriptures we'll find there are many that teach on the topic of prayer—that's how important it is to God that we talk with Him. Just as loving parents desire long distance calls from their children, God devised a plan that we could call on Him.

Inspiration #37

Putting Others First Can Impact Our Lives

"Love one another with brotherly affection (as members of one family), giving precedence and showing honor to one another."— Romans 12:10 (AMP)

There was one piece of cake left from the family celebration. It was a perfect slice. The strawberry filling oozed from between the two layers of the vanilla cake. It was topped off with a delicious, mouth watering chocolate frosting that was just the right touch to tantalize the taste buds.

I was saving it for my husband Jeff to eat, but he generously offered it to another family member so they could enjoy it, instead. My heart was touched by his decision to give up the tempting desert.

When we make the decision to put ourselves second, we are making the choice to allow others to be first and take precedence over our own desires. Have you thought about how you may have allowed someone to have precedence over your desires? It doesn't have to be anything great. Many times it's shown in the little things we do.

While grocery shopping we may be pressed for time. However, we notice someone standing in line behind us with only a few items in their cart. Despite our busy schedule, we make the decision to allow them to go ahead of us in the line.

While waiting in line to use a public restroom, we decide to allow someone who is handicapped or a parent with a small child to go ahead of us. These are just a few ways we can allow someone else to take precedence over our wants or needs.

Allowing others to be first, shows our selfless love, respect, and desire to put others first. Adjusting the way we may normally think and changing our focus from our own needs to meet the needs of another shows we care about someone else besides ourselves.

Letting someone's needs take precedence over ours in the little everyday matters is a small way we can make a big impact.

Inspiration #38

Procrastination Can Steal Our Opportunities

"But while they were on their way to buy the oil, the bridegroom arrived...And the door was shut."—Matthew 25:10 (NIV)

For that past 3 weeks, there has been something I have been meaning to do. However, I find myself putting it off.

Although I am not usually one to put things off, I find myself dragging my feet as the old saying goes. I'm even asking myself, "Why am I procrastinating about this?"

Have you found yourself putting something off until a later time? It happens to all of us from time to time. It may be something as small a task as emptying the trash can. But even a small delay eventually causes a stink.

Procrastination is like a thief in the night. It creeps up on us unexpectedly and steals something away from us. Holding off until a later time may cause us to miss, lose or delay an important opportunity.

In the Biblical account in Matthew 25, Jesus warns us of missed opportunities from putting something off. There were 10 women who were warned to prepare for the bridegroom. By trimming the wick on their lamps and keeping them filled with oil, they would be prepared to watch for him in case he arrived during the night.

Five of the women were wise and promptly did as they were instructed. The other five were foolish as they put off doing today what they felt could be done tomorrow instead. They procrastinated when it came to buying the oil for their lamps. When they finally got around to getting the oil, they missed out on going with their bridegroom because the he arrived while they had gone to prepare. The door was shut tight for that opportunity to ever take place.

The devil uses temptations such as procrastination to steal God-given opportunities from us. He convinces us that putting things off until tomorrow won't matter. But what we do today does matter. When temptations come to push something important aside, we need to remember the old saying: "Don't put off until tomorrow what you can do today."

Inspiration #39

Learning to Listen Is an Important Skill

"And all the people listened attentively."—Nehemiah 8:3 (NIV)

I was in the middle of a phone conversation with a friend when I found my mind drifting off thinking about the many things I had to do. I'm not sure how many seconds had passed when I realized I'd hardly heard a thing she said.

I was brought back into the conversation when she questioned, "Don't you agree?"

My mind raced for the right response. What would I say to her, "Uh, sure."

I figured I'd better respond in truth and ask her to repeat what she had just told me. After all, she may have said something vitally important. It was my responsibility to listen attentively.

Have you ever been caught in an embarrassing encounter like that? It happens to all of us from time to time. But at the end of this conversation, I felt like God was convicting me, "What if that was the way I listened to you?"

Oftentimes, we are well-meaning when we converse with others. However, our minds can wander off distracted by other things or our own agendas.

Learning to listen is just as important to our ability to communicate as talking. Many people want to do all the talking and monopolize the conversation. They simply pass it off as having the gift of gab. But wisdom means balancing our communication skills by being a good listener as well.

Lending a listening ear takes time, practice, patience and self-control. It's acquiring the art of listening from the heart.

A good listener might repeat the facts back in kind to assure the other person they've heard what's been said. As a nurse, I often did this with orders doctors would verbalize to me to ensure I got the facts straight.

In this busy day and age, we like to multi-task while communicating. Sometimes, it's appropriate to stop and sincerely listen to what someone has to say. And when we feel our minds drifting away during a conversation, it might be time to bring it to a close until we can control our wandering minds and give our full attention to what is being said.

I've heard it said that God gave us two ears and one mouth. Maybe we should give that some thought. It might be His way of showing us we were created to be good listeners.

Inspiration #40

Where Do We Put Our Trust in Troubling Times?

"Some trust in and boast of chariots and some horses, but we will trust in and boast of the name of the Lord our God."—Psalm 20:7 (AMP)

Have you considered where your trust is placed? From time to time, I like to examine who or what I trust. I wonder if I am putting an unhealthy trust in my friends, expecting too much from them. Or, do I trust in myself, leaning too much on my education, successes and possessions?

In these troubling times when the economy is shaky and so many things are uncertain, we need to examine where our trust is. Our trust belongs in God and His ability to guide and direct us and to help us handle problems and overcome them. Having the faith for Him to do what we can't do ourselves is a true test of our trust.

We all go through tests of our faith. The devil uses them as times for temptation to entice us to get upset and act in ungodly ways. God uses them to test our spiritual strength and faithfulness to Him.

Trust carries with it attributes that we can use as a measuring stick. If we can identify these characters or markers, they can help us discern to what degree we are using our faith.

According to Scriptures when trust exists, it doesn't get anxious and distraught trying to figure everything out. It stays stable, level-headed, and strong in the face of adversity, turning the worries and cares over to the Lord while continuing to perform normal daily activities. It leans on God to take control over the things we have no power to change, and prays for wisdom to make the changes we need.

Trust is a factor of faith. So if we remain faithful to pray, stand on the promises God gives us in the Bible and wait on God's timing, these factors can help us keep our emotions stable and our hearts faithful in the midst of troubling times.

Learning to trust God is a process. When storm winds blow, will keep we our faith in Him? I know I still need to grow, but I'm not giving up. How about you?

When we exchange our worry and fear, God gives us Peace and joy instead. Sounds like a great exchange to me. Take the challenge to lean on God and place your trust in Him.

Inspiration #41

Forgiveness Allows Us to Feel Better Instead of Bitter

"Bear with each other and forgive whatever grievances you may have against one another..."—Colossains 3:13 (NIV)

As a young woman, I learned a powerful lesson in unforgiveness. I hadn't spoken to my oldest sister for a few years. I wasn't angry at her. It was just our lives had taken us in different directions, and she had moved away.

A few years later, we were united again.

During a phone conversation she explained, "I forgive you for..." Then she mentioned something that had happened between us several years before. I never realized it was an issue for her. I hadn't even thought twice about it.

Then I realized how my sister's unforgiveness toward me, had caused her misery over something I knew nothing about.

I was free from any bitter feelings while she was bitter and miserable. She was being held captive in an emotional prison.

To forgive the other person doesn't always mean they weren't wrong. Some of the people we forgive may not know they've done anything wrong. Others may not be sorry for what they've done. It just means you are willing to stop being bitter over something you can't change.

God is our vindicator and only He can smooth out our issues. God instructs us to forgive because unforgiveness is unhealthy for us in many ways.

First, it is spiritually unhealthy because our spirits weren't created to be blocked with bitterness. Bitterness hinders us from full intimacy with God.

It is emotionally unhealthy because it blocks the emotions of joy and peace from freely flowing through our hearts and minds. Sometimes it causes disease because we are constantly under an emotional stress our bodies weren't designed to handle. Stress releases the adrenalin hormone, which increased on a constant basis can wear out our organs.

Forgiving doesn't mean we never bring correction to a situation or confront an issue. But regardless of the outcome, we choose to forgive what happened.

Although we may not feel like forgiving someone or something, we can make a decision to do so. We can voice our concerns to God and ask Him to help us. Even if our feelings don't seem to support our decision right away, if we keep turning the issue over to God eventually our feelings can catch up with decisions. Instead of being bitter we can find we're feeling better.

Inspiration #42

Search for Joy in the Midst of Work, Troubles

"Do not grieve, for the joy of the Lord is our strength..."—Nehemiah 8:10 (NIV)

The worries and fears of life's problems can drag us down.

If we keep our minds on our problems all the time, we can become problem-focused. Focusing on the problem only causes the worry and fear to intensify and stresses us.

God tells us worry weakens us, and joy strengthens us. Searching for joy in the midst of life's troubles always lightens our load and our relaxed state can help bring those solutions to mind.

Nehemiah was a Biblical prophet who was grieved over the destruction of the protective walls surrounding Jerusalem. Through prayer he realized it was his task to rebuild those walls. But in doing so, there was great opposition coming against him and his helpers. In the middle of the project they were feeling weak and weary.

One day, Nehemiah had a talk with his workers and instructed them that the joy of the Lord was their strength. Nehemiah and his workers decided to find the joy in their task working for the Lord and carried on with the job to complete it.

God has given us the emotions we need to get through the difficulties of life's trails. One of them is joy. But how do we find Godly joy that strengthens us?

The writer of the Biblical Psalms prayed, "Restore me to the joy of your salvation." (Psalms 51:12) This writer believed keeping our perspective that we have been given eternal life through God's plan of salvation in Jesus Christ fills our hearts with joy.

Thinking on the good things to be thankful for can turn our worries into joy.

Changing our facial expression by smiling can cause the our worried frowns and furled brows to take on a new body language thus making us feel better. Besides, we may get some smiles back in return. I believe Jesus smiled at people.

Laughing restores joy to a situation. Laughing at our silly mistakes can lighten our moods.

Playing with a child can make our hearts merry. Jesus enjoyed little children.

Helping someone in need fills our hearts with joy.

Praying with expectation to receive answers and relief can render a happier heart.

Like Nehemiah, as we take on the task to rebuild something in our lives, let's find the strength to do it through the discovery of Godly joy.

Inspiration #43

Those Who Give Generously Often Receive Rewards

"Give, and it shall be given unto you; good measure, pressed down, and shaken together, and running over, shall men give into your bosom. For the same measure that ye mete withal it shall be measured to you again."—Luke 6:35 (KJV)

My friend lifted up her head from her pillow, and found a clump of hair lying there. She gently picked up the strands and held them in her hand. She was saddened but not alarmed, however, for she knew it was a reaction to the chemotherapy treatment she was receiving for the treatment of her cancer. She was informed by the nurses that it was a side effect that she might expect.

With her positive attitude she pulled out one of her colorful scarves from the dresser drawer. She wrapped it around her head and started about her day. Besides, think of all the money she could save on mousses, sprays and cuts.

One day an idea hit her. She knew of a young man who was unemployed. He was placing applications all over town, but his shabby appearance might be a hindrance on a job interview. She knew she wasn't going to need to get a hair cut, so she gave the money for her hair cut to him, so that he could feel good about himself and look his best for a prospective employer.

A few days later, something wonderful happened. My friend received an unexpected check in the mail. The sender said it was to help her with her medical bills. Her bills had been mounting up and this was a big relief. Then she pondered how she gave to the young man that was in need. Now God was giving back to her more than she gave.

One of God's promises is that as we are led by the Spirit to give to others, He will give back to us. Now, there's no guarantee's as to when and how it will come back to us—and it does require we give with the heart attitude to bless.

I like to think of God's generous promise this way: a positive action positions us for a positive reaction.

When we're hurting we feel better by reaching out and helping someone else who is hurting. Regardless of our circumstances, each day we should be challenged to think about what positive actions we could plant into someone's life.

Inspiration #44

The Spiritual Practice of Self-Control Improves Our Lives

"Like a city whose walls are broken down is a man who lacks self-control."—Proverbs 25:28 (NIV)

Are you over-indulgent or impulsive? Do you think before you speak? Or do you just blurt out anything that's on your mind? Or do you need to have the last word?

Do you resist the impulse to buy something you don't really need? Or does that desire to add one more thing to your cart tug at your heartstrings before leaving the store, only to leave you broke and disgusted that you couldn't resist?

And what about passing up that second helping or the oversized portion of desert? Does it trap you every time?

If this is you, don't feel alone or ashamed. I'm not excusing the behavior, but all of us face temptations and are over-indulgent or out of control in some area of our lives.

Oftentimes, we can serve others too much. We can over-work. We can overexercise. Yes, even too much of a good thing is overindulgence as well. We all must work, eat, sleep, spend, exercise etc. but when we overdo it, we are headed for a path of destruction that depletes our energy and diminishes our productivity, relationships and true enjoyment.

The good news is the Lord Jesus Christ can help us break free of impulsive behaviors through the use of self-control.

Self-control is a spiritual attribute deposited deep within the believer. It's not mere will power or wishing. It's actually God's power within ourselves to give us the strength we need to exercise self-control in our lives.

We don't actually lack self-control, we just lack the use of it. A self under control takes responsibility for their own actions, and doesn't place the blame on others. Looking at what self can change and control is no more than controlling our own attitudes and behaviors—not those of someone else.

Self-control helps us make decisions about money, time, relationships, etc. based on practical principles we can learn rather than just following the pleasurable desires of our culture.

Practicing the use of a controlled life helps us feel powerful, not powerless as we yield to God's help and not merely our own. It helps us to improve our lives as we overcome destructive obstacles and develop our greatest potential to succeed and live a life of joy.

Inspiration #45

What Does it Mean to Be Holy?

"Who is like you—majestic in holiness ..."—Exodus 15:11 (NIV)

Each Sunday, many people across our nation attend church to worship God and learn more about Him. Congregations gather together to hear sermons that challenge our thinking and the choices we make. The melodious music played by organs, pianos, horns, or stringed instruments can stir the emotions of our hearts to be reverent out of gratitude or joyous over God's mighty miracles.

I remember one particular moment as a young girl, when I stood by my pew along with other church members, and sang the lyrics of a favorite hymn.

As I sang the chorus, an emotion of joy arose from within my soul. However, as I sang out the words, "Holy, Holy, Holy" regarding God, I suddenly wondered what I was singing about. I'd heard and sang these words many times before, but this time was different. I pondered what this word "holy" meant.

Part of our spiritual journey is to grow in understanding of the things and the ways of God. Although we can never understand all there is to know, if we are really on the path to spiritual maturity we will desire a deeper understanding of the knowledge of God. By defining meanings of the words from the Bible, it can enlighten our spiritual understanding and help us in our process for growth.

At this moment, you might be wondering what is means to be

holy. Simply put holiness means to be pure or without sin. God is the only one who can meet those requirements. But He invites us into a lifetime process of becoming holy as well. This first happens through our faith in Jesus Christ. Then for us to be holy signifies a separation unto God. We have a heart that desires to please Him and to follow His example, rather than our sinful nature. Then little by little, throughout our lives, through our determination and God's strength we can be separated from those sinful desires toward the ways of God.

When our heart's desires are right, we can begin to see positive changes in our behavior and thoughts. We can be led by our heart's passion to follow a holy God and be guided into God's purpose and plan for our life.

Inspiration #46

Live, Love, Laugh Your Way Through Good Times and Bad

"You have made known to me the path of life."—Psalm 16:11 (NIV)

My day started off like any typical day. However, about mid morning, my daily routine was interrupted by a phone call.

A family member was calling to inform me that my oldest son's close friend had died.

I was stunned by the information that this vibrant young man, still in his 30's, was no longer alive. I hung up and called my son to offer some loving support and see how he was taking the news.

After conversing with him it was hard to concentrate on my work. But by early afternoon, I figured it was time to get going. However, once again, the phone rang. I picked up the receiver and detected the quiver in my friend's voice, as she informed me that her husband's test results were conclusive for cancer.

I could hardly believe all the sad news. It felt as if some huge dark cloud was looming overhead. Then a package containing something I had ordered a week before arrived at my door.

I opened the box to remove three wall plaques containing the words, "Live, Laugh, and Love." As I read them I thought to myself, "What a timely reminder, Lord."

Life is here and gone. To live a full life, we need to remember how important these key components are.

How do we "live"—by trusting God to help and strengthen us. We pray for God's plan to be fulfilled and that He guide our paths. We look for things to be grateful for and express our gratitude. Remember not to blame God. He doesn't cause our adversity, He helps see us through it. We Pursue God's principles and wisdom to make wise choices.

The Bible refers to "laughter" as medicine for our body and soul. During times of stress we need to de-stress by finding ways to tickle our funny bone even though it seems there is nothing worth laughing about.

According to the Scriptures "Love" is the most excellent way to live. It's a vital force to a life that excels. A person with a loving heart shows mercy and compassion. They apologize quickly and give of their time, talent and finances. Love does the right thing not to receive rewards or accolades from others, but simply because it is the right thing to do.

Living, laughing, and loving keeps us on the right path on any given day.

Inspiration #47

Be Patient While You're Waiting for God's Answers

Let be and be still, and know (recognize and understand) that I am God—Psalm 46:10 (AMP)

I use to manage a doctor's office. As I walked through the waiting room, I observed that each patient had a different method of waiting. Some people sat thumbing through the pages of a magazine. Other patients paced back and forth, unable to sit still. Some sat wringing their hands. After waiting only a short time, others gave up and left. Many came to the desk and complained that they had to wait. This activity gives us an example of how we wait in most of our circumstances.

Right now as I write this to you I am in God's waiting room. I am waiting on some answers to prayer.

You may be sitting in His waiting room too. As we submit our plans, requests and concerns to God in prayer, He asks us to take a seat, and be still until the answers come.

It is difficult to wait for "The Great Physician" to answer a problem that is eating away at our minds and emotions. But, He asks us to be still and wait, because He is working on things that don't make sense to our human reasoning. When our emotions take over, we don't always make good decisions. I think about the patients that left the doctors office due to their impatience. What complications may have arisen because they wouldn't wait long enough to allow the doctor to treat their ailment?

To “let be and be still” doesn’t mean that we never do anything. Being passive or lazy is not what God is referring to. He wants us to be still from worry. And to let be from taking matters in our own hands and utilizing wrong ways of handling them. He is also teaching us patience. I believe the quicker we learn these things, the shorter our waiting time may be.

Our Heavenly Father, has promised to take care of us. If we could understand God’s timing we could better co-operate with Him. If we are going to walk in obedience to God and enjoy His blessings, we have to learn to let go of our timing and our ways and allow God to bring us something far greater than we could imagine, but in His time.

Inspiration #48

Attend Your Local Church

"Let us not give up the habit of meeting together..." Hebrews 10:25 (TEV)

Some people wonder what church is all about. I'd like to share a few of the various reasons I have found for meeting together with other believers. Attending church can heal a lonely heart. Getting involved in church activities and meeting with other people who have the same spiritual values can bring us out of feelings of isolation.

There is nothing like the power of many people gathered together in prayer to cement our relationship to God. Being united in prayer provides a special sense of connection that we can only experience gathered among other believers. Listening to the Word of God presented in a way that can be applied to our lives, can help us formulate new values that are counter to the current immoral standards of our culture. Allowing the message to soak into our memory banks can change the way we think and give us a new outlook on life. Over time, it can improve the way we make my decisions. Singing in unison with fellow believers can fill our hearts with worship that relieves a heavy and burdened soul. Scriptures inform that God inhabits the praises of His people. Lifting our voices in praise fills the room with presence of God.

Serving others at church can give us the opportunity to use talents and abilities we might not use somewhere else. Teaching, singing, supporting are among a few. Through serving others we can discover the joy of giving of ourselves. Formulating relationship with other believers can give us Godly advice and the support we need to make good choices. Fellowship helps us face life's difficulties.

Bible study from an educated leader can give us spiritual insights we may not discover on our own. The various benefits received from going to church will spill over into our daily lives and bring about a blessing.

Inspiration #49

Expect the Unexpected

"For your thoughts are not my thoughts, neither are your ways my ways."—Isaiah 55:8 (NIV)

God's ways are unexpected. When we are waiting for something in our lives, a healing, a new mate, or a problem we need resolved, we start thinking about how it should come about. But how God plans to make this delivery to us can be different. He showed me this regarding a simple matter.

I was expecting a book in the mail I had ordered. I was excited to receive this book, so with each day's mail delivery I was anxiously awaiting its arrival.

One particular day after the mail delivery, I saw my book had still not come. For a brief moment, disappointment set in. I figured I would have to wait one more day. However, a few hours later, a UPS truck pulled up and a man came to my door with a small brown package in his hand.

It was my book. I never expected it to arrive that way! After all, it was small enough to fit in my mailbox, why should it be delivered UPS?

What God showed me that day was whatever we are waiting for, it's not in our way, or our expected time of arrival…it is in His unexpected ways.

Inspiration #50

Dust off Disappointment

"When people do not welcome you, shake the dust off your feet when you leave their town as a testimony against them."—Luke 9:5 (NIV)

I sent an e-mail to a friend. I put in the subject line—"Prayer request for a disappointment." She quickly responded to me, "I had a disappointment today, too." I started thinking how disappointment is a part of life.

In Luke 9:5, Jesus was taking His earthly experience of disappointment and giving His disciples heavenly advice. He was no stranger, to disappointment. People rejected His ministry, and denied His existence continually. Now He was instructing the disciples that people and circumstances would disappoint them, and when this happens, they should shake off the dust of rejection and go on.

The last few years, God has been teaching me a lot through life's disappointments. I have seen disappointment's regarding my health, relationships, and career. He has shown me that each one brings a challenge to try harder, or to make a change, because He has a new plan for my life.

However, this requires that I make a choice and take action. I must shake off the dust of my old thoughts and attitudes, to find a new beginning.

I am learning to overcome disappointment by implementing a battle plan. As a writer if I get a rejection letter, I rewrite my piece and resubmit it to another editor. (I have had success doing this too!) As I look to be healed from my illness, if there is no redirection, I try to enjoy where I am and I pray for strength to get through the day.

God is gently whispering to us all, He understands our feelings. However, remaining stuck in disappointment is not His way. He knows we can't live the abundant life He has waiting for us, if we are sitting in the dust of our disappointment. Working with Him, through the acceptance of change and praying for His direction, is what turns our emotional dust into gold dust!

We overcome disappointment by allowing Him to lead us to a new golden door of opportunity, when those old doors tightly close.

Inspiration #51

Refuse to Have a "Pity Party"

"How long will you mourn for Saul, since I have rejected him as king over Israel? "—1 Samuel 16:1 (NIV)

I just finished reading the words, "How long will you mourn?" I was deeply convicted by them. I realized all I was doing day in and day out, was mourning over my losses. I had turned a normal time of grief into an unhealthy way of dealing with my losses.

I had become bitter and angry over my rejected circumstances. I was longing for all the things I no longer had, my job, my relationships and perfect health.

God instructed me to write. But I was stuck in a rut of feeling sorry for myself. I was spending my time having a 'pity party' with the demon of self-pity, while I lingered in my bed or sat in my chair and cried a river of tears.

When I continued reading the rest of the verse, I realized once again, I was living by unhealthy emotions. "Fill your horn with oil and be on your way, " where the words that echoed through my mind.

Oil is symbolic for the anointing of the Holy Spirit. God was telling me that I was anointed to do something and I better get to it. I realized that I needed to stop feeling sorry for myself. Instead, I became determined to do what God instructed me to do, which was to write.

Each morning I got out of bed and started writing the devotions that were flooding my soul. When the days came that I wanted to stay in bed with my old partner 'Mr. Self-pity,' I told myself I wouldn't have that party today. I refused! I would get up and call a friend and have a positive conversation, or play some upbeat music and praise God for the good things I had left. As I got my behavior in agreement with what God instructed me to do, I started to feel better about myself and my desire and creativity to write started to increase. I found myself excited to get up in the morning.

We all grieve disappointments, however, there is a time for grief to end. God instructs us to powerful. That means through the power of His Holy Spirit we can utilize self-control over unhealthy emotions that drag us down. Not giving in to them makes us feel more powerful and more joyful. We can enjoy life when we refuse to attend 'pity parties' on a regular basis.

Inspiration #52

Be Honest with God

"I do believe; help me overcome my unbelief!" Mark 9:24 (NIV)

My son called me with disappointment in his voice. He had been employed with a company for several years that promised to help him reach his goals. Now, a new company had taken over the business and he found himself facing the loss of his dream. He was unemployed and uncertain about his future. He had his heart fixed on a particular career direction. But closed doors started causing him to doubt if God was hearing his prayers regarding this issue. He wondered of God existed.

"Mom, I want to believe that God is here," he said. "But I am just not sure I do."

"I understand that feeling," I reassured him. "We have all been there. Just be open and honest with God, and tell him how you feel. He will help you out."

Then I remembered the Bible story in Mark, chapter nine, about a boy who needed healing. His father approached Jesus, "I do believe; help me overcome my unbelief!" I felt prompted in my heart, to tell this story to my son.

"Mom, that is exactly how I feel! He replied to me with great excitement in his voice. This Scripture gave him the reassurance that he was not the only one that ever felt doubtful.

A few weeks passed by, when my son called me with some

exciting news. A new job prospect he hoped for was opening up to him. He received an interview with this new company. He was the job and immediately, was given the opportunity he had awaited the last company to provide him. His dream was restored. He couldn't believe how God answered his prayers.

God wants our belief, but He also wants our honesty. The man whose son needed healing went before Jesus with a heart of true honesty that moved the Lord to answer his prayer.

We must strive to grow in our faith. But, during difficult times when we can't, we need to simply go before God with an honest heartfelt request... "Lord, I do believe; help me overcome my unbelief!"

Conclusion

Do you feel like what you want is beyond your reach? At times, I have. During those times I like to meditate on this passage of Scripture: "What I am commanding you is not difficult or beyond your reach."—Deuteronomy 30:11 (NIV)

Keep reaching out to God today for His help. Be patient and know your dreams are not beyond your reach!

Invite Jesus In

If you have never invited Jesus into your life to give you eternal and abundant life, you can do so by saying a simple prayer of faith. If you feel at loss for words, fill your heart with faith and let me help you.

Heavenly Father, I come to you and confess that I believe Jesus died for my sins. I ask for forgiveness and to be filled with your Holy Spirit. Take my life and do something miraculous with it. In Jesus name I pray.

My Statement of Faith

I believe in the trinity, The Father, Son and Holy Spirit. That Jesus Christ is the only way to heaven. "I am the way and the truth and the life. No one comes to the Father except through me." John 14: 9 (NIV)

About the Author

Annettee Budzban is a registered nurse who found a new purpose during a time of disability.

Her first spiritual experience happened when as a young girl she felt the tug of the Holy Spirit speaking to her heart and she received Jesus Christ as her Savior.

As she continued life's journey she married just before her seventeenth birthday and shortly thereafter, became a teenage parent. Sadly, that fifteen year relationship ended in divorce, and she took the journey of a single mother and raised 3 teenage boys on her own for nine years. She knows what it's like to have sick children, lose parents to death, experience the grief of loss of relationships, career and health.

At the height of her nursing career a change of plans due to an illness, opened her up to a deeper spiritual search. Her search for a deeper love for God and His direction, brought an unexpected marriage and a call to write. During her illness she had to give up her active nursing career but through Divine inspiration of the Holy Spirit, started writing her syndicated newspaper column, *Inspirations.*

Through her varied experiences and losses she has learned to live victorious by applying practical Biblical principles to her life.

With God's help, Annettee has gathered all the fragments of her past experiences and uses them in her new purpose.

During her 18 year nursing career she spent 8 years in varied nursing positions and 10 years in leadership as a nurse manager and educator.

As an entrepreneur she established and promoted her own business in childbirth education. She has taken her knowledge as an entrepreneur and childbirth educator and transferred her skills to start the ministry: *Be Inspired!*

She now enjoys helping others though writing, speaking, Bible teaching and one-on-one life coaching to birth their God-given dreams and visions.

Today, she desires to share her inspirational Biblical view to instruct and inspire others to conquer life's adversities through the power of Jesus Christ. She enjoys helping others conquer patterns of defeat and bring them into a place of wholeness, healing and strength using God's word.

If you're interested in any of her many books, hearing her speak, or moving forward through a one-on-one coaching session, Annettee can be contacted by e-mail at AnnetteeBudzban@aol.com or you can visit her website AnnetteeBudzban.com

CPSIA information can be obtained at www.ICGtesting.com
Printed in the USA
LVOW111916210212

269782LV00001B/1/P

9 781591 291343